STEM IN BASEBALL & SOFTBALL

CONNECTING
STEM AND SPORTS

STEM in Auto Racing
STEM in Baseball & Softball
STEM in Basketball
STEM in Extreme Sports
STEM in Football
STEM in Gymnastics
STEM in Ice Hockey
STEM in Soccer
STEM in Track & Field

Southern High Media Center
Harwood, MD 20776

CONNECTING
STEM
AND SPORTS

STEM IN BASEBALL
& SOFTBALL

AIMEE CLARK

MASON CREST
PHILADELPHIA · MIAMI

Mason Crest
450 Parkway Drive, Suite D
Broomall, Pennsylvania 19008
(866) MCP-BOOK (toll free)

First printing
9 8 7 6 5 4 3 2 1

ISBN (hardback) 978-1-4222-4331-2
ISBN (series) 978-1-4222-4329-9
ISBN (ebook) 978-1-4222-7475-0

Cataloging-in-Publication Data on file with the Library of Congress

Developed and Produced by National Highlights Inc.
Editor: Andrew Luke
Interior and cover design: Annalisa Gumbrecht, Studio Gumbrecht
Production: Michelle Luke

QR CODES AND LINKS TO THIRD-PARTY CONTENT

TABLE OF CONTENTS

CHAPTER 1 THROWING 9

CHAPTER 2 HITTING 17

CHAPTER 3 CATCHING 29

CHAPTER 4 RUNNING 37

CHAPTER 5 THE STATS 45

CHAPTER 6 THE EQUIPMENT 57

CHAPTER 7 NEXT-GEN TECH 67

Series Glossary of Key Terms...76

Further Reading & Internet Resources 77

Index...78

Author Biography & Credits 80

KEY ICONS TO LOOK FOR:

Words To Understand: These words with their easy-to-understand definitions will increase the reader's understanding of the text while building vocabulary skills.

Sidebars: This boxed material within the main text allows readers to build knowledge, gain insights, explore possibilities, and broaden their perspectives by weaving together additional information to provide realistic and holistic perspectives.

Educational Videos: Readers can view videos by scanning our QR codes, providing them with additional educational content to supplement the text. Examples include news coverage, moments in history, speeches, iconic sports moments, and much more!

Text-Dependent Questions: These questions send the reader back to the text for more careful attention to the evidence presented there.

Research Projects: Readers are pointed toward areas of further inquiry connected to each chapter. Suggestions are provided for projects that encourage deeper research and analysis.

Series Glossary Of Key Terms: This back-of-the-book glossary contains terminology used throughout this series. Words found here increase the reader's ability to read and comprehend higher-level books and articles in this field.

INTRODUCTION

Casey Jones, Babe Ruth, Cy Young, Lou Gehrig, Sammy Sosa, Barry Bonds, and Jackie Robinson all have one thing in common. They are all expert users of STEM (Science, Technology, Engineering, and Mathematics) skills.

Okay, they are also all legends of the game of baseball. However, every great baseball and softball player uses the skills and methods of STEM. It may seem unlikely that these areas would interact, but the fact of the matter is neither baseball nor softball would be possible without science, math, and even engineering. Furthermore, new advances in technology are moving these sports into a whole new area in the twenty-first century.

The interactions cross several areas and are often surprising to consider as an aspect of what is largely considered an athletic activity. From the physics of throwing the ball to the mathematics involved in the statistics used throughout Major League Baseball (MLB) to the engineering and technology behind creating perfect balls, helmets, and other gear, STEM and baseball are intertwined. Don't forget the science of running, swinging, and power hitting. Even looking into the future, new gadgets and technology propel the game ever forward like a juggernaut.

Far from being dumb, so-called jocks often use complex scientific concepts and other STEM-based ideas without even realizing it. Teams now hire coaches to teach players to intentionally employ the math, science, engineering, and technology of baseball.

Read on to learn how they do just that.

WORDS TO UNDERSTAND

aerodynamics: the traits of an object that influence how effortlessly it is able to move through the air

drag: the impeding force acting on a body moving through a fluid or gas—like air—parallel and opposite to the direction of motion

lift: the upward motion created by the aerodynamic force of an object as it moves through the air

torque: the inclination of a force to change or cause the spin of an object that is calculated by multiplying distance and force

velocity: the direction and rate of the change in the location of an object

CHAPTER 1

THROWING

The Science behind Pitching

There is a whole lot more to throwing a baseball than just . . . well, throwing the ball. Physics and **aerodynamics** are part of every pitch. Through these two scientific concepts, the ball is moved effectively over the 60 feet and 6 inches that stretch between the pitcher's mound and home plate. During that journey— or any journey for that matter—the forces of **lift**, **drag**, and gravity affect the ball.

Gravity is a pretty simple concept because it is always bullying the

Pitchers use a windup to get as much velocity on the ball as possible.

baseball down toward the ground, much like it does with the spilled popcorn and discarded peanut shells that litter the stands after a game. **Lift** counters the effect of gravity as its upward motion moves the ball skyward. **Drag** comes in the form of wind resistance as the ball flies through the air toward its target and works with gravity to bring that ball back to the ground.

A baseball, or softball, needs a considerable amount of energy to make it across home plate so pitchers use a windup to put enough force on the ball to do that. This windup uses the largest muscles (those in the lower body) first. Thus, when the pitcher releases the ball it has the force of more than an arm alone can provide.

THE WORLD'S FASTEST PITCH

According to the *Guinness Book of World Records*, the fastest baseball pitch ever thrown by a man was clocked at 105.1 miles (169.1 kilometers) per hour. It was thrown during a game at PETCO Park in San Diego, California. Cuban-American pitcher Aroldis Chapman threw the stunning fastball. He was the pitcher for the Cincinnati Reds in a game against the San Diego Padres on September 24, 2010. For reference, the average speed of a baseball thrown in MLB is roughly 92 miles (148.06 kilometers) per hour.

More than manipulating speed alone, pitchers use a further understanding of physics and aerodynamics to control how the ball rises, turns, or sinks at the last possible second. These moves create a further challenge for batters that goes beyond the speed and strength of the pitch alone.

This is where the unique engineering and design of the ball itself comes into play. The distinctive seams that hold each baseball together also serve to create the wind resistance that pitchers use to create the sinking, rising, and side-to-side motion of the baseball. It all relies on where the pitcher places his hand on the ball when it is thrown.

Fastballs are thrown to overpower batters so that they swing late and miss. They are thrown with the first two fingers of the hand resting on the seams. The less contact with the ball the fingers have, the more off-speed, or slower than expected, a pitch will be. Although all pitches are thrown with the same arm speed, less finger contact

The way the pitcher grips a baseball determines the type of pitch that is thrown.

means less **velocity** and **torque**. Velocity is the pitcher's arm speed coupled with the force exerted, determined by turning the palm of the hand as the ball is released.

Torque is how the pitcher "twists" the ball toward or away from the batter at the last second. The pitcher adding an intentional spin to the ball as it leaves the hand creates torque. These minute differences result in different pitches.

Sinkers are off-speed pitches that—as the name says—sink as they near the target. Screwballs are another form of off-speed pitch that also does just as its name says, twisting like a corkscrew and causing it to break away from or toward the batter.

Breaking pitches are those that—surprise, surprise—break either toward or away from the batter, like the corkscrew. They vary from the cutter (which breaks only slightly) to the curveball (which uses topspin to increase the severity of the break).

These concepts are all aspects of the science of physics. Since a ball needs quite a bit of energy to overcome the force of gravity, it is essential to understand these concepts and how to use them to get the ball exactly where it needs to be. This is the most essential concept for pitching, but it is

A Discovery News discussion on the science of pitching.

just as important for outfielders and others who throw the ball to understand as well.

The most essential concept around pitching is that how the ball responds to gravity is determined by the amount of energy transferred to it.

Outfield Assists

How in the world can a center fielder throw the ball the 200 feet between the outfield and second base to get a runner out? It is all about the physics and geometry—yep, math!

As with a pitcher, an outfielder needs to consider the physics of force, lift, drag, friction, and energy. In addition, this player needs to consider the angle at which they throw the ball to maximize the distance and land it securely in their teammate's mitt.

The force of the throw begins the ball's forward motion. Drag and gravity simultaneously slow the progress of the ball and pull it downward. For that reason, the ball must be thrown up and out at an angle. The degree of this angle and the amount of force put behind the throw are what will determine whether the ball falls short, soars past, or lands squarely in the glove of its target.

Players make it look easy, but it takes a lot of practice to master the force and knowledge of angles needed to consistently make accurate throws.

The ball moves through the air in the shape of a parabola, which is a type of mathematical curve. Too sharp of an angle with too little force results in a flat curve, which will have the ball hitting the ground before it reaches its target. Conversely, too wide an angle coupled with excessive force will send it sailing over the head of the player who needs it. The throw could go wrong in many ways. However, careful understanding of the mathematics of angles and the physics of aerodynamics gets the ball where it needs to be every time.

The Technology That Is Changing Pitching

One of the elements that most marks the twenty-first century is the advent of innovative technologies. It seems like every day some new advancement or discovery is made. Throwing in the games of baseball and softball is not immune to this.

Over the more than 100 years since MLB's inception, the athletic ability of people in general has changed. To continue to be relevant, the game itself has had to change as well. Although professional baseball is often considered a game that rarely changes, it does, in fact, morph to suit the times, from changes in the height of the pitching mound to the addition of artificial turf.

The future of baseball may include modern innovations such as the following:

- A pitch clock—The delay between pitches has grown incrementally over the decades. Today, the pace of the game suffers from these delays by adding more than ten additional minutes to each game. To keep the attention of fans, MLB has considered adding a pitch clock that limits the amount of time a pitcher has to throw the ball, much like the play clock in American football or the shot clock in basketball.

Automatic strike zone technology may one day replace one of the biggest parts of an umpire's job – calling balls and strikes.

- Automated strike zones—Although they will never completely replace umpires, these high-tech devices electronically define strike zones, making them more exact. They also automatically detect whether or not a pitch is a strike. No longer would strikes and balls be judged by eye but rather by automated technology.

- Mobile apps——There are smartphone applications in development to help players improve their throwing or pitching. One app records not only pitch velocity but also movement and location, providing a metric for pitch accuracy. A separate application works in conjunction with a sensor worn on a pitcher's arm to track the workload put on the arm. This information can be used to monitor and control the progression of young pitchers or to improve overall performance while tracking potential issues to reduce risk of injury.

Throwing the ball is not the only area where technology is making changes in the games of baseball and softball. Technology continues to be a large part of the entire game.

Text-Dependent Questions:

1. What two aspects of STEM learning are used in throwing the ball in baseball and softball?

2. How does a pitcher control the rise, fall, and side-to-side motions of the ball that are designed to trick the batter?

3. What is the difference between the fastball, off-speed pitches, and breaking pitches?

Research Project:

With all other factors—speed and force of the throw, wind resistance or drag, gravity effects, time of day, etc.—considered to be equal, construct a graph, chart, or some other physical representation of how far a ball will travel when thrown at three to five different angles.

WORDS TO UNDERSTAND

acceleration: the rate of change in velocity of an item per unit of time

angle: the figure formed by two rays – the sides of the angle – that share a common endpoint known as the vertex

kinetic energy: the energy that an object possesses due to its motion

mass: the amount of material in an object

momentum: the property of a moving object to resist stopping

CHAPTER 2

HITTING

Swing Science

Hitting a baseball moving at more than 90 miles per hour from 60 feet away is an amazingly difficult feat. The average fastball thrown by pitchers in Major League Baseball (MLB) is traveling 90 mph or more and spinning roughly 20 times a second. That means the ball is coming in fast and hard.

Even in softball, where the ball is thrown at slower speeds and a larger ball is used, the ball still comes in at dangerous speeds. However, due to the dynamics of the larger softball, that upper register is around 80 to 85 mph.

The batter has a little more than half a second to decide what to do. That is how long it takes the ball to travel from the pitcher's hand to the batter. Snapping your fingers takes longer than that! It is literally the length of time it takes an eye to blink.

In that tiny amount of time, the batter must assess what pitch was thrown and decide whether to swing. Further, they must ensure that their grip on the bat and the **angle** at which they hit the ball is conducive to a great hit.

Batters have about half a second to make a decision after the pitch is thrown.

The key to a great hit is to match the right swing angle with the pitch thrown. Hitters who can predict what pitch is coming have the advantage. As do those hitters that can see the ball while still in the pitcher's hand. Knowing how they are holding the ball can give an important clue as to which pitch they will throw. With either of these, the hitter gains a few valuable milliseconds to adjust their swing to meet the ball at the proper angle.

Hitting the ball with a bat tilted to different angles produces distinct kinds of hits. With all other factors remaining constant, the necessary angle for a particular hit is:

- ◇ Grounder = less than 10 degrees

- ◇ Line drive = between 10 and 25 degrees

- ◇ Fly ball = between 25 and 50 degrees

- • Most professional players consider a fly ball hit at an angle of 45 degrees to be optimal for the chances of hitting a home run.

- ◇ Pop up = more than 50 degrees

Where the bat strikes the ball affects its direction. For example, if you hit a ball in the middle of the plate dead center then it will likely head straight back toward the pitching mound. However, if the bat strikes higher on the ball than its midpoint, then the ball with be sent toward the mound on the ground, or go over the

Swinging the bat at the correct angle can turn fly balls into line drives.

pitcher's head if the point of contact is below center. Hitting the ball at the proper angle and in the proper place will allow the batter to control where the ball goes, how far in that direction it goes, and the height of its flight.

There is yet more science and math involved in hitting the ball.

The Sweet Spot

Every bat has an area that makes the ball go farther than other spots on the bat. This is due to vibrational physics. Hitting the ball on this "sweet spot" ensures that the maximum **momentum** will be transferred to the ball. Thus, the ball will fly the furthest.

When a bat is struck by a ball, the ball pushes the bat sideways slightly and makes it bend. This bend is imperceptible to the naked eye but is observable via slow-motion cameras. When the bat unbends it creates a vibration that can be felt by the batter. When the sweet spot is hit, there is no vibration. Thus, the **kinetic energy** that would have been wasted on that movement is transferred to the ball.

While momentum and kinetic energy may seem to be the same thing and in fact, are closely related concepts in the physical sense they are distinctly different. Momentum is a vector quality meaning that it is directional while kinetic energy is scalar meaning that it is not dependent on direction. For example, to say that somebody is walking 3 miles per hour is a description of a scalar quality while applying a directional element to the movement by saying that somebody is walking 3 miles per hour to the south is a description of a vector quality.

Finding the Sweet Spot

To locate the sweet spot on a bat, follow these simple steps:

⟫ With arm extended, hold the knob of the bat loosely between the thumb and fingers.

⟫ Have another person gently tap on the dangling bat with a hammer starting in the middle of the bat and progressing downward.

⟫ As they tap, vibrations will travel up the bat and into the fingers of the person holding it.

⟫ When they no longer feel vibrations, mark that spot. That is the sweet spot.

Power Hitting

Speed and power are causally related. Power is simply a measure of kinetic energy and how that energy is shifted to the ball upon contact. It includes the factors of **acceleration** and **mass**.

The speed at which the bat is traveling when it hits the ball is a key factor in how hard and far the ball travels. The ball compresses to approximately half of its normal thickness when it is squarely hit. This compression is short lived as the ball only has around one thousandth of a second of contact with the bat.

The power applied to the bat during the swing by the body and hands is measured in watts. An increase in applied power allows the bat to reach its maximum momentum faster. In addition to sending the ball the maximum distance, this also allows the batter to swing later and reach maximum acceleration. This provides the batter with more time to assess the pitch and swing accordingly.

Using a bat of the proper weight will ensure maximum acceleration is possible. With a heavier bat, the batter expends more power to swing, and that increased power is then transferred from the batter's body to the bat and then the ball. However, if the bat is too heavy, the barrel speed—also commonly known as "bat speed"—will drop. Therefore, it is essential to find a bat that is heavy enough but not too heavy.

The speed the hitter is able to generate with the bat is a major determinant of how far the ball will go when hit.

Righty vs. Lefty

Left-handed batters are considered to have an advantage over right-handed batters. But why?

When there is a runner at first base, lefties can more naturally hit a ground ball between second base and first base through the infield. It is more natural for batters to hit to the side they are batting from, known as pulling the ball. For the lefty, this means that a ground ball hit between first and second has a chance to get through with the first baseman holding the runner. Right-handed batters have to try and hit the ball the opposite way from their natural swing to take advantage of the opening in the infield.

Another reason left handed batters have an advantage is that they are literally one step closer to first base. The momentum of the swing also takes them in the direction of first base. The opposite is true for right-handed hitters. Right-handed hitters have to take one extra step as they run to first base, and their momentum takes them the other way. This one step (roughly one sixth of a second) may be the difference in reaching the base before the opposition tags them out. Fast lefties make infielders work harder for that out.

Hitting is one of the most difficult feats in modern sports. The pros make it look easy, but that is all part of their amazing athleticism.

The math shows that left-handed pitchers have the advantage over left-handed hitters compared to right-handed hitters.

Finally, since the majority of pitchers are righties, this means that left-handed batters naturally have an advantage in most at-bats. When facing a pitcher throwing with the hand opposite to how they are batting, the batter has the advantage of seeing the baseball better when the pitch is coming. As Washington University professor David Peters explains, "A right-handed batter facing a right-handed pitcher actually has to pick up the ball visually as it comes from behind his (the batter's) left shoulder. The left-handed batter facing the right-handed pitcher has the ball coming to him, so he has a much clearer view of pitches." The principle

Right-handed batters tend to do better against right-handed pitchers than left-handed batters do against lefties.

holds true for lefties facing left-handers as well, but there are far fewer left-handers.

It is common for managers of the team at bat to bring in left-handed batters to face right-handed pitchers—and vice versa—in key situations to negate these advantages as much as possible. The math supports this strategy. In 2012, for example, left-handed batters had a batting average of .232 versus left-handed pitchers, but .260 against righties. Right-handed batters did not have quite as big an advantage, hitting .251 versus righties and .263 against lefties.

The Ideal Bunt

When a batter bunts they hold the bat still and let the ball hit it. This produces a ricochet effect and the ball bounces to the ground somewhere between the batter and the pitcher. However, there is more to bunting well than simply holding out the bat.

Every skilled bunt involves reducing the energy of the ball after it hits the bat. A poor bunt will likely reach a fielder rather quickly and then the batter is thrown out. Batters need to slow the momentum of the ball. To do this they must understand the science of the ball and bat interaction.

Ideally, a bunt will have just enough momentum to roll about halfway down either baseline.

If the batter waits until right before the ball reaches the bat and then tilts the head of the bat back slightly then the bat will absorb some of the pitch's energy. This deadened bunt results in a ball that travels a shorter distance.

However, this ball will still roll back toward the pitcher. To avoid this and give the batter an advantage, the batter must employ angles to his or her benefit. The batter needs to angle the bat to direct the ball either to the left or to the right. He or she also needs to intentionally hit the ball off the sweet spot using the lower part of the bat's barrel. This helps to control the ball and reduces the distance it will go. Therefore, the ideal bunt is one that deadens the ball, angles it toward the ground, and directs it between the pitcher and either baseline.

All of this is known because the people that loved and lived the game used physics, math, engineering, and technology to push the game further than it has ever gone.

Text-Dependent Questions:

1. What ways can a batter improve their swing?
2. What is the difference between momentum and kinetic energy?
3. Why does the "sweet spot" make the ball fly farther?

Research Project:

Partner up with another person and conduct an experiment with deadening the ball. Find the sweet spot of your bat first so that you can avoid that area throughout the experiment. Try different angles and areas of the bat and record how far the ball flies. Try to get as close as you can to dropping the ball at your feet. Create a graph of your results to present orally.

WORDS TO UNDERSTAND

arc: moving with a curve trajectory

Newton's First Law: an object at rest will remain at rest until acted on by an outside force and an object in motion will remain in motion until acted on by an outside force

probability: the degree to which an incident is likely to occur, calculated through the ratio of the promising cases to the entire number of probable cases

trajectory: the path followed by a flying projectile or the object that is moving under the action of some outside force

CHAPTER 3

CATCHING

Catching a ball may seem like a relatively simple task. However, that could not be further from the truth. Physics plays a large part in every aspect of catching, including the construction of the glove. Just grabbing a ball out of thin air that is flying at speeds that average 100 miles per hour with your bare hand is not only exceedingly difficult but dangerous.

The catcher's glove is an integral part of the game and is designed to absorb the impact of a speeding pitch. The pocket that lies between the index finger and the thumb functions as a place for the ball to lose speed without injuring the player's hand. The larger surface area of that pocket provides the hurtling ball surface area to dispense its force upon. It even expands to allow the ball to slow down faster.

The Physics of the flight of the ball. There are several forces at play on a baseball – it goes well beyond just the pitcher and the hitter.

Based on **Newton's First Law**, the ball would remain in motion until acted on by the force of the catcher's glove.

The Science behind Outfield & Infield Catches

As for catching, it is difficult to explain the human ability to estimate the **trajectories** of balls moving at 100 miles per hour on average. The best fielders start moving as soon as the ball cracks against the bat. They estimate where they believe the ball is headed and position themselves to be under it. Due to the speed of the ball, the fielder may have to dive or leap to catch it. A dive occurs when the fielder has underestimated the velocity of the ball. A leaping catch takes place when the ball is flying at a higher trajectory and may be heading to home run territory.

Fielding requires extensive coordination of the body, eyes, and brain. Two of the leading scientific theories on how baseball and softball players do it are Optical Acceleration Cancellation (OAC) and Linear Optical Trajectory (LOT).

The catcher's mitt absorbs the force of the ball, causing it to no longer be in motion.

A physicist at Stanford University developed the concept of Optical Acceleration Cancellation theory. According to OAC, fielders track in a vertical dimension that requires them to move forward and backward to keep the ball within a part of their field of vision that is roughly at a 45-degree angle to the ground.

Fielders use Linear Optical Trajectory to track balls in the outfield.

As the ball leaves the bat, the fielder tracks the ball as it rises into their field of vision. If the fielder were to stay in place and the ball is hit hard enough to go over their head, the fielder would track the ball as it rose until it was directly above them or at a 90-degree angle. If the ball landed in front of the fielder, they would see the ball rise and fall without their viewing angle rising above 45 degrees.

Linear Optical Trajectory was developed out of OAC theory to describe the process that a fielder uses to follow the path of a batted ball. LOT states that the fielder must adjust their movement toward the ball so that its trajectory follows a straight line through their field of vision. Rather than compute the landing point of the ball, racing to that spot and waiting, the fielder uses the information provided by the path of the ball to constantly adjust his path so that they intersect at the right time and place.

Both LOT and OAC argue that the fielder repositions throughout the flight of the ball to keep this viewing angle between 0 and 90 degrees. If it rises too fast, the fielder needs to turn and run backwards. If the viewing angle is low, then they need to move forward so that the ball does not land short.

Fielders cannot always make it to the landing spot in time but keeping the ball at about a 45-degree angle by moving will help ensure that they get to the correct spot to catch the ball. While OAC explained balls hit directly at a fielder, LOT helps add the side-to-side dimension.

The best outfielders position themselves to have forward momentum when they make a catch so they can step into a throw if needed.

There is a reason why the best fielders catch the ball while moving forward. They can then use the momentum and kinetic energy of their forward motion to throw the ball to the player that needs it to make the play. This added energy helps the velocity of the ball along the **arc** with which the fielder threw it.

Buster Posey — The Best Catcher in the Majors

Buster Posey of the San Francisco Giants is baseball's best signal caller. Posey is a former NL Rookie of the Year, the 2012 NL MVP, and a six-time All-star through his first 10 seasons. He also won the NL

Gold Glove in 2016 for being the best fielder at his position. Posey is also a master pitch framer. In 2016, He had 213 of 277 close pitches called as strikes, a better than 3:1 ratio, and by far the best in baseball.

The Math behind Calling the Game

The catcher initiates almost everything in the game. From the first pitch to the final out, the catcher's call starts it all. This player must know all the pitchers and their little idiosyncrasies. If they do, then they will be able to recognize when a pitcher is excelling or struggling with a certain pitch on a particular day.

In addition, the catcher needs to have a feel for the rest of the game. They should be aware of the tendencies of all of the opposing hitters and track how the hitters are swinging the bat, moving their feet, and tensing their body. That can signal what type of pitch they are prepared for and the catcher can order up a different pitch to throw the batter off.

While paying attention to all the parts of the game, the catcher must use **probability** to predict how the pitcher, batter, runners, and fielders are going to react. Weighing the percentage of the chance that something will either happen or not happen—known as situational probability—requires split second math skills. The catcher then uses these situational probabilities to direct their team mates.

For example, on a 3–2 pitch with a runner on first, the catcher must weigh questions such as:

◇ Which pitch has the highest probability of inducing a swing?

- In this situation where there are already two strikes, a pitch such as a curveball or one that otherwise dives, turns, or

Framing pitches is a tactic that catcher's can deploy if they are aware of the probabilities that certain umpires may be more likely to be influenced to call a strike.

moves at the last second is most likely to induce both the swing and the third strike the defensive team wants.

» What is the probability that a runner will steal a base?

- With two strikes, it is highly probable that the runner on first will attempt to steal a base. Most pitcher/catcher teams will forego trying to hold the runner leading off in an attempt to get that third strike which will negate any stolen base.

» What is the tendency of an umpire to call a strike on a pitch framed on the outside corner?

- Since the umpire's view of the outside corners are often obscured by the catcher's body, getting the umpire to call a strike on a pitch framed there depends largely on the performance of the catcher. As long as the catcher acts quickly, the umpire may call a strike even if it may not actually be one.

All of these calculations and evaluations must run through a catcher's mind in a split second. Calling the wrong pitch, framing the pitch poorly, or giving away the pitch's location early can be the difference between winning a game and losing.

Math guides the game, physics propels the ball, and new advances in technology help it to evolve over time.

Text-Dependent Questions:

1. How does arc affect the trajectory of the ball?

2. Which ball is more likely to go farther, one that is thrown at a 90-degree angle or one that is thrown at a 45-degree angle? Why?

3. How can probability be used to predict how other players will behave?

Research Project:

What are Newton's other laws of physics and how do they apply to the game of baseball? Write a detailed, thoroughly researched explanatory essay that covers this topic.

WORDS TO UNDERSTAND

center of gravity: the point around which an object's weight is evenly distributed

reaction time: the interval of time between receiving a signal and activating a response

response: a physical reaction to a precise situation or stimulus

stimulus: something that evokes a reaction, whether voluntary or involuntary, in a person, especially appeal, exhilaration, or physical action/reaction

variable: a factor, feature, or element that is liable to change or vary

CHAPTER 4

RUNNING

The Science Behind Reaction Time

Reactions and reflexes seem to be similar on the surface but are, in fact, quite different. Reflexes are completely involuntary and are thus, faster than reactions. While it may seem like professional or other highly skilled baseball players are acting on reflex they are carefully reacting to what is happening around them. Often, making split-second calculations is almost like a reflex.

This rapid consideration of the elements around them is how a baseball or softball player develops a skilled **reaction time**. This conscious decision is what makes up the **response** and whether it is the right one or not often depends on the reaction time. Sprinting between first and second to steal a base is only effective if the reaction time to the **stimulus** is swift.

When a play is made, the baseball or softball player takes in all the visual stimuli present and processes it. Once a decision is made on how to proceed, the brain then sends the signals to the muscles needed to initiate that decision. When they burst forward in a run

The reaction time of the base runner to the beginning of the pitcher's motion is a big component of base stealing.

they continue to process how the game around them is changing and adjust accordingly. The reaction times of most major league players are utterly amazing.

Reaction time is something that is learned through years of practice and a complete understanding of the game. As the game has progressed so have the average reaction times of its players. They have even learned a few tricks along the way to speed things up even further.

Billy Hamilton—Fastest Runner in Baseball

The Cincinnati Reds' center fielder Billy Hamilton has been established as the fastest runner in Major League Baseball. His speed is undeniable even to the naked eye. In addition, a look at the stolen base leaderboard supports that observation. However, the advent of tracking technology has eliminated any doubt by providing concrete data to support the twenty-five-year-old player's claim to fame. During the 2018 season for example, Hamilton ran from home to third base in 10.83 seconds, the fastest time of the season. On the play, Hamilton covered a blistering 29.8 feet per second.

Sliding in to Base

Sliding in to a base head first is one of those things.

As a player rounds second base and races toward third to beat the throw, every fraction of a second counts. Using physics, it has been proven that diving in to a base (a headfirst slide) is moderately faster. One of the reasons for this is that it allows the feet to give an extra push on the dive to gain fractions of a second.

However, the most vital part of why headfirst slides are faster has to do with the player's **center of gravity**. While where this is located on each person varies, it is always somewhere in the lower abdomen. When a player dives at the base they are throwing their center of gravity forward which generates extra momentum.

Conversely, when a player slides into the base feet first, they are simply dropping their center of gravity on the ground which impedes forward momentum, causes more friction, and therefore, results in slower movement. Still, many players prefer to slide into a base feet first to make it easier to jump up if the play does not end at that base for some reason and they are less likely to hurt their valuable batting and catching hands.

At first base, however, the option exists to run through the base, and traditionally players are taught it is faster to do this than to dive. Diving eliminates all acceleration and introduces friction, both of which can be avoided by running through. The debate continues as to which method is best at first base, with influencers like former University of Illinois physics professor and technical advisor Alan Nathan coming down on the side that diving can be faster. That dive, however, would need to be perfectly timed, which makes running through the more practical option.

Base Running Angles

An old adage says that the fastest route between two points is a straight line. The baseball and softball diamonds encourage this

A feet first slide is slower because it drops the center of gravity and causes more friction.

concept with their straight baselines between bases and if a batter is only going to make it to first base then that is true. However, several studies have shown that in baseball and softball, at least, it is not a constant. Enter geometry and its crazy angles and arcs again.

As far as baseball is concerned, if the batter hits a double, the fastest—and still legal—route takes a path that arcs. Starting from a resting position at home, the batter launches forward on a path that veers out at an arc of 28 degrees from the baseline. Once they have hit first base they make another 28-degree arc to second. On average, it takes runners about 10.4 seconds to leg out a double following this path. Sticking to the baselines takes 12 seconds.

Using those same metrics, a run for home should also be run on an arcing path rather than along the baselines. However, the angle should be adjusted down to 25 degrees from home to first. This path shaves more than five seconds off a runner's time versus sticking to the baselines.

Those seconds could be the difference in making it home safe. Slower runners may be stalled at second, or worse, tagged out between the bases.

For softball, it might seem that the angles and arcs would be different. This is due to the fact that while there is 90 feet between bases on a baseball diamond, that distance is much shorter on softball diamonds. Even the largest of these only has 60 feet between bases. However, despite the different distances, the angles and arcs hold constant for both the baseball diamond and that of softball.

The Physics and Math of Stealing Bases

Stealing a base is a simple concept that involves complex physics and mathematical equations. It is something that the best base burglars calculate in their heads almost automatically. The factors involved are logical: the time from one base to the next must not be more than the time for the pitcher to deliver the pitch added to the time it takes the catcher to throw to the base being stolen.

The distance between each base is 90 feet (27.43 meters). By dividing this distance into five components, researchers have broken down how to determine what are the most

Taking the optimal base running angles can reduce the time it takes to run from home to second base by nearly two seconds.

important aspects of the stolen base. These five components in order of importance to a positive outcome when attempting to steal a base are:

◇ The runner's top speed reached during the run.

◇ The acceleration of the runner at the beginning of the run.

◇ The runner's speed when reaching the stolen base.
 (A headfirst slide might be necessary here.)

◇ The distance of the runner's lead off the base they are leaving.

◇ How fast the runner can stop running and hold contact with the stolen base.

With these many **variables**, it is easy to see why stealing second base is not something that happens often; but that is not the only impediment.

The catcher and pitcher have a lot of input into whether a stolen base is successful. The catcher has to quickly transfer the pitched ball from the glove to the throwing hand and accurately throw it to the correct infielder.

Education and entertainment combine as ProSwing Baseball host Matty Maher breaks down three ways to run to first base.

Baseball experts have long contended that the pitcher's role is the most important in stopping a steal. The time of their throw to the plate is ideally 1.3 seconds or less while the catcher's average speed to second base is roughly 1.85 seconds. If a runner can make it from first to second in that small window of time, then they may just be able to steal a base.

Obviously, the best counts to run on are those when the probability of a pitcher throwing breaking balls and change ups is highest. Off-speed pitches take about 1.6 seconds to reach the

Pitchers are wary of base runners, especially when the count is statistically favorable for the runner to attempt to steal.

Base stealers try to hit their top speed in as few strides as possible.

plate. For most pitchers this will be when they're ahead or even in the count (0-1, 0-2, 1-1, 1-2, 2-2).

MLB scouts know how long it takes each pitcher to deliver to the plate and each catchers timing to throw to second. If teams know their own runners' steal times it becomes a simple math solution in given situations. If, for example, a pitcher has a 1.6 second delivery time and the catcher takes 2 seconds to throw the ball to second, it is a high-percentage play to send a runner who typically gets to second in 3.5 seconds or less.

Text-Dependent Questions:

1. Why is headfirst sliding faster than feet-first sliding?

2. What is the difference between reflexes and reaction time?

3. How should a runner run the bases if they hit a double?

Research Project:

Grab your thinking cap, your imagination, and your research skills and find other examples of the use of center of gravity in the world. Then build an example, construct a poster board display, or find another way to demonstrate what you learned.

GIANTS VS. BREWERS   8/8/00   Pac-Bell Park

No.	BREWERS	POS.	1	2	3	4	5	6	7	8	9	10	11	AB	R	H
10	Belliard 2B			◇	◇		◇		◇	◇		◇	◇	4	0	0
9	Grissom CF			◇	◇		◇		◇	◇		◇	◇	4	0	0
5	Jenkins LF			◇	◇		◇		◇	◇		◇	◇	4	0	0
11	Sexson 1B		◇		◇	◇		◇		◇	◇	◇	◇	3	0	1
20	Burnitz RF		◇		◇	◇		◇		◇	◇	◇	◇	3	0	0
18	Hernandez SS		◇		◇	◇		◇		◇	◇	◇	◇	3	0	0
2	Houston 3B		◇	◇		◇		◇	◇		◇	◇	◇	3	0	0
12	Blanco C		◇	◇		◇		◇	◇		◇	◇	◇	3	0	0
21	Wright P / 25 Casanova PH		◇	◇		◇		◇		◇	◇	◇	◇	3	0	1
			◇	◇	◇	◇	◇	◇	◇	◇	◇	◇	◇			
			◇	◇	◇	◇	◇	◇	◇	◇	◇	◇	◇			
			◇	◇	◇	◇	◇	◇	◇	◇	◇	◇	◇			
	TOTALS	R/H												30	0	2

PITCHER | IP | H | R

No.	GIANTS				R	H
7	Benard CF				0	0
32	Mike Mueller				0	2
25	Bonds R				0	0
21	Kent 2B				0	1
6	Snow 1B					0
23	Burks				0	1
35	Aurilia S				0	0
19	Estalella C					
48	Ortiz P / 52 Crespo PH				0	
	TOTALS					6

WORDS TO UNDERSTAND

algorithm: a process for solving a mathematical equation in a fixed number of steps that frequently involves repetition of an operation

average: a number that expresses the typical or central value in a data set, particularly the median, mode, or mean that is found by dividing the sum of the values by the number of data sets

metric: the standard for evaluating or measuring something using average and figures

sabermetrics: an application of statistical methods to analyze baseball stats to compare and evaluate individual player performance

statistics: the scientific practice of collecting numerical data in copious quantities for analysis to extrapolate proportions of representative samples to the whole

PACIFIC BELL PARK
(HOME OF THE SAN FRANCISCO GIANTS)

PITCHER | IP | H | R
Ortiz | 7 | 2 | 0
Rodriguez | 1 | 0 | 0
NEN | 1 | 0 | 0

CHAPTER 5

THE STATS

Statistics and the mathematical algorithms that they use are as essential to the game of baseball as are the bat and ball. Managers use them when choosing the players for their teams. Coaches use them to inform the team's strategy. Even fans use statistics when they are talking up their favorite players. These stats come in a wide variety and have largely ambiguous names with acronyms such as WPA, wOBA, and OPS.

Every baseball card has the players stats on the back. From pitchers to outfielders and every position in between, statistics shape which players are revered, and which are forgotten to history.

Statistics for Pitchers

The Baseball Hall of Fame has more inducted pitchers than any other position. This may be because much like the quarterback in football, the pitcher serves as the leader of the team. The position stands

Earned Run Average is the most commonly tracked statistic for pitchers.

out from the rest due to how much control this player has over the game.

Earned Run Average (ERA)

The most commonly known stat for pitchers is the Earned Run **Average** or ERA. It records the average runs a pitcher would allow to occur in the standard nine innings pitched. This demonstrates how well the pitcher is preventing the opposition from scoring. The algorithm that is used to determine ERA is:

Runs Allowed ÷ Innings Pitched × 9

The ideal in the modern era is an ERA below 4.00. The average ERA of Major League pitchers in 2017 was 4.36, which was the highest in ten years. The ERA splits into two categories: lifetime ERA and season ERA. The first covers the pitcher's entire career ERA statistics and the season ERA is recorded for each year in which the pitcher plays.

Pitcher performance is measured by the statistic known as WHIP, which is Walks + Hits/Innings Pitched.

The lowest recorded career ERA in MLB history belongs to Ed Walsh. Walsh played for both the Chicago White Sox and the Atlanta Braves during his thirteen-year MLB career (1904 -1917). He only allowed an average of 1.82 runs per game.

Tim Keefe—also known as Smiling Tim—has the lowest recorded season ERA of 0.86 runs allowed per game. He played for four different teams during his thirteen-year career from 1880 to 1893; the Troy Trojans, New York Metropolitans, New York Giants, and the Philadelphia Phillies.

Jennie Finch, a two-time Olympic medalist and collegiate softball champion, had a career ERA of 1.08 runs allowed per game. She is just shy of being part of the National Collegiate Athletic Association (NCAA) Division I softball career sub-1.00 ERA list, that—as its name suggests—lists NCAA pitchers who have a career ERA of less than 1.00.

Walks & Hits per Inning (WHIP)

Another statistic that guides and shapes Major League Baseball is the Walks and Hits per Innings Pitched (WHIP) **metric**. This metric is often used along with the ERA, and shows how well a pitcher keeps runners from reaching base. It follows a simple formula.

All hits count as one. Not just singles but also doubles, triples, and home runs. This number is then added to the number of walks the pitcher allowed. The total is then divided by the number of innings the pitcher throws. Thus, the formula for WHIP is:

(Walks + Hits) ÷ Innings Pitched

This metric—like ERA—can indicate how well a pitcher is doing his or her job. The job of the pitcher is not simply to throw the ball but to keep the other team from getting on base. Pitcher is a position on the defensive roster after all.

Wins (W)

This is the most basic of stats. Or so it would seem. However,

In softball, wins and losses are attributed to pitchers, but are not a very accurate reflection of how a pitcher is performing.

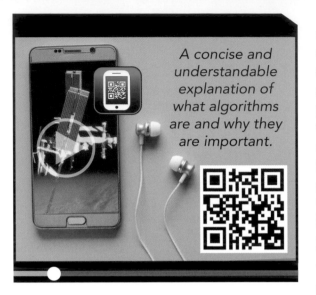

A concise and understandable explanation of what algorithms are and why they are important.

understanding what counts as a win can be a bit confusing. Each game can only have one pitcher credited with the win regardless of how many pitchers pitched in the game and helped get the win. So now there has to be a metric by which the deserving pitcher is assessed.

The determining factor is taking the lead and not giving it up. This means that the pitcher who takes the W (win) is the one who is pitching when their team takes the lead and then that pitcher has to ensure the opposing team never takes it back. Furthermore, the starting pitcher cannot earn a W unless they pitch five complete innings.

Today's pitchers do not throw for anywhere near as many innings as the pitchers of Major League Baseball history. Cy Young—who played from 1890 to 1911—is the overall leader in wins with 511. It will be hard for any pitcher today to beat that record.

Statistics for Hitters

There are several algorithms used to determine which hitter is the best. Like those for pitchers, the metrics for many of them are similar with slight variables or changes. The most commonly cited stat for hitters is the Batting Average.

Batting Average (BA)

While the most common, this stat is dismissed by some of today's statisticians. It is quite simple, the number of hits a player gets is divided by the number of times the hitter was at-bat.

Batting Average = Number of Hits ÷ Number of Times At-Bat

The result of this equation is then rounded to the nearest thousandth. This stat is also split into career and season totals for recording. It is said as if there is no decimal. This is a stat that has been around since nearly the beginning of professional baseball. Some newer stats are taking some of the bluster from Batting Average.

On-base Percentage illustrates how successful a player is at reaching base, and considers all means of doing so in the calculation.

On-Base Percentage (OBP)

Similar to Batting Average, this stat goes deeper to show how successful hitters are in reaching base, which is, of course, the only way they can score runs. Managers often use this to choose their leadoff hitter. OBP focuses on more than hits, it includes: walks (aka, Base on Balls, BB) and number of times hitter hit by pitcher (HBP). It also takes into consideration the number of At-Bats (AB) and Sacrifice Bunts (SF).

The algorithm used to determine this stat is:

(Hits + BB + HBP) ÷ (AB + BB + HBP + SF)

This stat gives a good picture of how well a hitter is playing. Managers and scouts look for high OBPs when they are assessing hitters.

STEM Careers in Baseball— Statistician

Statisticians are indispensable in the sport of baseball. Beyond what the Oakland A's did during the *Moneyball* seasons, statistical analysis affects every aspect of baseball from the hiring of players and managers to what kind of stadium a team should build.

Combined with a love of the game, a statistician can have a promising career in baseball. This career is not limited to working for a specific team; large sports media networks such as ESPN, Sports Illustrated, and Fox Sports employ statisticians.

Slugging Percentage (SLG)

This statistic shows the total number of bases a player accumulates per at-bat. This stat is useful for those power hitters that may not have as high a BA (Batting Average) as other players, because it does not treat all hits equally. The formula is:

Slugging Percentage = [singles + (2 × Doubles) + (3 × Triples) + (4 × Home Runs)] ÷ AB

Extra base hits are weighted more heavily to better illustrate in one number the kind of hits a player is getting.

On-Base Plus Slugging (OPS)

One of those new statistics that statisticians have created by observing the previous two is the On-Base Plus Slugging Stat. Researchers have determined that combining OBP and SLG can give a more accurate picture of a hitter's overall production than either of the others do separately.

OPS = OBP + SLG

Hall of Famer Hank Aaron has a career slugging percentage of .555, which is in the top twenty of all time in Major League Baseball history.

Sometimes advanced math comes in the form of simply adding two numbers together to get an overall solution to the problem. Babe Ruth holds the best career OPS with 1.1636 while Barry Bonds claims the best season OPS with 1.4217 in 2004 when he played for San Francisco Giants.

Sabermetrics

At its core, **sabermetrics** is simply the pursuit of unbiased data about baseball. It is named after the Society for American Baseball Research (SABR), which has worked for decades to refine the way we evaluate how the game is played. While the analysis of baseball statistics has existed since the beginning of competitive play, SABR often questioned traditional stats that were used to evaluate players—like wins and ERA for pitchers or batting averages—and worked to develop more meaningful alternatives. This left it mocked and ignored for years, until people realized that sabermetrics made sense.

Some of the advanced metrics that sabermetrics added to the game include:

World Series champion Mookie Betts led MLB in Wins Above Replacement for the 2018 season.

⟫ Weighted on-base average (wOBA) – Designed to measure the total offensive contributions of a player per appearance at the plate, it is reached by:

- Run values of all offensive events ÷ appearances at the plate = # then scaled similarly to OBP (On-base Percentage)

⟫ Fielding-independent pitching (FIP)—This statistical analysis converts the three possible outcomes of a pitch into a stat similar to an ERA number. It is reached by:

- Home runs × 13 + 3 × (HBP + BB) – 2 × strike outs) ÷ Innings Pitched = plus a constant of roughly 3.2 so that it is on the same scale as ERA

⟫ Wins above replacement (WAR) – This is a sabermetric approach to summarizing each player's total influence on their team all in one handy stat. It is often used to indicate how many more wins the individual player is likely to contribute verses a replacement. The formula for WAR depends on the position being evaluated.

Primarily, sabermetrics is a science that follows the scientific method that dictates conclusions must be based on logic and evidence. Further, if new evidence is found that contradicts those conclusions, they can be reconsidered and, if necessary, overturned.

Moneyball—The Math & The Movie

The 2011 Brad Pitt movie *Moneyball* highlights the inside workings of baseball. It gives its viewers an inside look into the behind-the-scenes action of Major League Baseball (MLB). More specifically, it is an exposé of Oakland A's manager Billy Beane and his 2002 method—based in statistics—for evaluating players. Beane's theories were based on those of baseball analyst Bill James, who joined other professional baseball statisticians and ushered in sabermetrics. These theories changed the game of baseball forever.

Fielder Stats

The fielders have statistics that are used to measure how well they do their jobs. The dominant one is their Fielding Percentage.

Fielding Percentage (FP)

This metric measures the number of successful fielding plays (putouts (PO) and assists (A)) against the total number of fielding chances, including errors (E).

FP = (PO + A) ÷ (PO + A + E)

A putout is making any out—catching a fly ball, catching the ball at a base, tagging a runner, etc. An assist means getting the ball to another player who makes the out. Errors are assigned if a fielder makes a mistake while attempting a putout or assist.

Fielding percentage indicates the percentage of plays a fielder executed properly out of all the player's fielding opportunities.

Managerial Statistics

While baseball managers are using stats to evaluate how well the players are doing their jobs, statisticians developed a statistical avenue to assess how well the manager is doing his or her job. There are several categories of information that a manager can be rated on, including:

- ⟫ How often the manager goes to the bullpen
- ⟫ The number of lineups used in a single season
- ⟫ Win/loss record
- ⟫ Rates of bunting, stealing, pinch-hitting, etc.

All of these factors and more go into algorithms developed by statisticians to determine a manager's style. Certain teams work better with specific managerial styles, and team owners can use this statistical data to help them hire the right manager for their team.

Stats keep the game evolving and growing so that it can keep up with the world in which it is played and adored. Modernization is a part of every aspect of daily life whether it is noticed or not. Statistics and probability play a large part in that modernization.

Text-Dependent Questions:

1. What does a batting average indicate?

2. Name three statistics used to evaluate pitchers.

3. Name two elements used to evaluate a manager's style.

Research Project:

Using statistical methods, build a Major League dream team. Using stats like OBP, ERA, WPA, etc., select players to fill every position needed on a Major League Baseball team. Research the players most recent stats, analyze the data, and choose players based on the algorithms that seem most important. Teams will face off in a statistical "game" of baseball to see who wins.

aluminum: a whitish silver metal that is malleable, light in weight, and ductile, and that does not easily tarnish and/or corrode; most often used in alloys to make lightweight and cost-effective airplane and car parts, utensils, baseball or softball bats, and other castings

biochemical engineer: a scientist that uses the principles of engineering, chemistry, and biology to improve current items and invent innovative objects in areas such as; biopharmaceuticals, biopolymers, industrial enzymes, and biofuels, among others

engineering: Other than being the "E" in STEM, this is also the creative employment of science, mathematical methods, and technology for the purpose of innovating, designing, constructing, operating, and maintaining processes, machines, systems, devices, structures, and materials

innovation: the process of creating and ushering in new methods, ideas, and devices or the devices, ideas, and methods themselves

CHAPTER 6

THE EQUIPMENT

The Engineering behind the Glove

As anyone who has ever caught a ball with his or her bare hand knows, the glove is an essential part of the game. It allows the fielders to handle the force of a 90-plus mile-an-hour ball. St. Louis Cardinal pitcher Bill Doak designed a rudimentary pocket between the index finger and the thumb in 1920. This ingenious pocket gives the ball a larger surface area upon which to distribute its force without hurting the player's hand.

The glove is an ideal example of an item that was born out of necessity. Pitchers in the early

The modern baseball glove has come a long way in the past century, but it is still the player's most personal tool.

years caught balls with their bare hands. The pain of doing so compelled them to start wearing leather gloves that were much like those that people wear in the winter today. Those gave way to thicker versions to allow more padding and then became the well-padded, webbed, widened gloves that are used today.

The Unsung Hero of Baseball and Softball Equipment

There is one piece of baseball/softball equipment that every team in MLB has but is often forgotten as being just that. While it has guidelines like other equipment, the team that calls it their own uniquely creates this important piece. It is the home field of that team's stadium or diamond, as it is called in baseball. Open air or enclosed will make a difference based on the effect wind has on the game. So will the location of the team's field, as different altitudes make a major difference in the physics of the game. Another key factor is whether to use natural grass or artificial turf. Turf is made with materials that allow the ball to bounce whereas the natural grass–covered ground absorbs some of the ball's energy. The different choices made when constructing a team's home field can make a world of difference in the physics of the game.

The Tech Behind Baseballs

The original baseballs consisted of yarn wound around rubber with a horsehide cover sewn around it. Of course, in these first days of the sport, balls were often made by players. Not surprisingly, they did not bounce well and lost their shape before the end of the game as rubber is dense and the covers were often poorly stitched.

Luckily, in early 1900, cork took the place of the rubber in baseballs. It has more spring than rubber does and caused fewer fluctuations in the weight of the ball. Around that same time, engineers developed machines to wind three layers of wool around that cork center. A polyester and cotton yarn layer is now added to the ball before it is finally covered with bleached white cowhide and stitched together with waxed thread that is distinctively red.

For the Major Leagues there are extremely strict **engineering** guidelines for the five to six dozen balls that teams go through during a game. In addition to the rule that those red wax stitches number exactly 108, these guidelines include:

⬦ A circumference between 9 and 9.25 inches (23 and 23.5 centimeters).

⬦ A weight between 5 and 5.35 ounces (142 and 149 grams).

⬦ Must regain its shape within 0.08 inches (0.2 centimeters) when pressed.

⬦ Must bounce back at 51.4 to 57.8 percent of the starting speed when thrown at a solid wood surface.

It may seem like these are extreme restrictions. However, the fact is that the shape of the ball is one of the biggest factors

Baseballs used in the Major Leagues are constructed to exacting standards.

affecting fastballs – the most common pitch – and is therefore, central to the game. The stitches cause additional friction with the air and have an important impact on the path of ball. The force acting on a ball due to this friction and the rotation is similar to that which acts on the wing of an airplane.

Major League Baseball takes these carefully created guidelines so seriously that in 170 years nobody has ever been able to create a machine to stitch the 108 red wax stitches into the cowhide cover properly. Thus, every ball is hand stitched by workers at one company in Costa Rica.

Bats

Another area where MLB adheres to strict engineering guidelines is bats. However, before these rules were implemented, players made their own bats much like baseballs. The variety of different bats that were whittled by

In softball and amateur baseball, aluminum bats are used. This high-tech piece of equipment is not permitted in MLB.

players to suit their own burgeoning ideas of how the physics of baseball worked was nearly endless.

Often, they were long and heavy. At that time, the idea was that a bigger bat meant more mass behind the swing and thus, a harder hit. Bats that weighed 20 ounces (567 grams) more than today's average and were in excess of today's average length by as much as 10 inches (25.4 centimeters) were commonplace.

The Major League Baseball rulebook gives the specifications for allowed bats:

⟫ Smooth, round stick

⟫ No more than 2.61 inches (6.63 centimeters) in diameter at the thickest point

⟫ No more than 42 inches (106.68 centimeters) in length

⟫ One piece of solid wood

This entirely excludes **aluminum** bats from MLB play. There are two reasons that developed out of scientific observation of the aluminum bat which excludes it from swinging in the majors. They have been used in lesser levels of play including college baseball.

The first reason that MLB bans these

Learn a few tips on what to look for in selecting the right baseball bat.

bats is for the safety of the players on the field. Aluminum bats are hollow and therefore, they give when hit by a fastball rather than compressing the ball. This means that more of the pitch's speed is maintained in the flight of the ball after hit. While this sounds great it can result in injuries to players who may get hit with the faster line drives aluminum bats provide. In softball—where aluminum is commonly used—this retention of speed is essential to help the larger, heavier, less compact ball fly a good distance.

The desire to maintain the human skill aspect of Major League Baseball over the skill of technological advances is the second reason that aluminum bats are banned. That desire does not exclude all advances of technology into the game. Quite the opposite in fact. The age-old game of baseball changes every year based on new data, new sciences, and **innovative** technologies.

STEM Careers in Baseball – Biochemical Engineer

In the early years of Major League Baseball (MLB), an injury often meant the end of a career. Luckily, sports medicine has come a long way since those days. That is thanks in large part to **biochemical engineers**. These are the scientists that developed breakthrough medications to allow athletes to return to baseball even after severe injury or sickness.

In addition, biochemical engineers are the ones who design safer helmets, more effective gloves, and better shoes for running. Moreover, they are the ones who develop the advanced nutritional information that helps athletes become the best version of themselves that they can be. Without biochemical engineers, the world of baseball would still be wallowing in the mediocrity of outdated equipment, nutrition, and medical treatments.

Modern batting helmets are designed using a light but tough carbon fiber composite.

The Tech of the Batter's Helmet

Just as the old-time players learned the hard way to wear a glove when catching a ball zooming at them, the players at bat took a few balls to the head before coming up with the idea to wear some sort of protective headgear. Sadly, it took the death of Cleveland Indians shortstop Ray Chapman in 1920 to start the drive for helmets that would prevent that tragedy from happening again.

Still, it was not until 1971 that MLB required their use and 1983 before ear flaps were added. The helmet went through many metamorphoses—like the glove—as new data and a better understanding of the causal relationship refined the helmet's design. The latest of these evolutions came in 2013 when

Baseball shoes are designed to give players traction on the dirt base paths and on the slippery grass of the outfield.

engineers introduced a revolutionary helmet that can protect the batter from the force of a fastball going 100 miles (161 kilometers) per hour.

This new helmet design utilized a new aerospace-grade carbon fiber composite to manufacture an outer shell that is light but provides a durable surface to absorb the impact of pitched balls. By absorbing and displacing the vast majority of the energy contained in a professionally thrown ball, the helmet casing protects the player's head without adding excessive weight or bulkiness.

There is no telling exactly where future innovations will take the batter's helmet.

The Tech of Spikes & Shoes

The Major League Baseball Rulebook specifically says that shoes with pointed spikes that are similar to track or golf shoes are not allowed. Thus, the Sports Engineers put their heads together and came up with spikes on the bottom of baseball cleats that are rectangular. There is still some debate over what the best material for cleats is: metal, plastic, or rubber. Softball players also have cleats on their shoes for traction.

Plastic cleats are considered to be easier on the players' feet. They hit fewer pressure points, are lighter, and distribute the players' weight better. Rubber cleats are slightly heavier than plastic but proved a durable, effective, and strong shoe. Metal cleats are heavier and harder on the players' feet but provide improved traction as they dig into the field.

New innovations in shoes and other baseball equipment help it march forward as the world progresses.

 Text-Dependent Questions:

1. Which are better, aluminum or wood bats? Why?

2. Which is better, grass or artificial turf? Why

3. What is the most important piece of protective equipment for baseball players?

 Research Project:

Using materials found around the house, make your own baseball. Try to make it as close to the requirements put forth by the MLB rulebook as possible. Test it using the "press" and "bounce" methods and any others that seem logical. Record the results and present them along with the ball.

WORDS TO UNDERSTAND

generation: the average period, roughly thirty years, during which people are born, grow up, reach maturity, and have kids of their own

technology: a branch of learning and knowledge that deals with applied sciences and engineering, as well as, the tools, devices, and machines created through application of that learning/knowledge and used to solve real world issues

Virtual Reality (VR): the simulated environment that is three dimensional and generated by a computer that can be interacted with to simulate a genuine experience

CHAPTER 7

NEXT-GEN TECH

Tech for Giving Fans a Better Experience

Due to the rapid advancement of internet-based **technology** for everyone, today's baseball fans are used to having instant access to whatever they want to know. To keep their fan base interested, Major League Baseball needs to keep up with the ever-changing landscape of social media and mobile applications for smart devices.

Livestreaming of Games & MLB.tv

For a prolonged period, baseball fans did not have access to the same coverage of their favorite teams as NFL (National Football League) fans. Sunday afternoon and Monday night armchair quarterbacks could root for their favorite teams and even pretend to be a manager with their own Fantasy Football league. That was before MLB.tv and live streaming of the league's 162 games.

Now, most baseball fans can follow their favorite team through livestream broadcasted games, real-time updates on changing stats, and much more. Even the online fantasy sports league world has opened up to Major League Baseball and its fans.

These advances and others promise to create a whole new **generation** of baseball fans.

Virtual Reality

Beyond Major League Baseball's TV channel and game streaming, MLB Advanced Media (MLBAM) is a compelling technology company that has its hand in many areas. In addition

With today's technology, it is possible to livestream your favorite MLB team's games to any device almost anywhere around the world.

to working for businesses like the NHL (National Hockey League) and HBO, among others, MLBAM develops video games, builds websites, and is a pioneer in the **Virtual Reality (VR)** world.

Recently, it has concentrated on increasing the game of baseball's fan base by putting enthusiasts into the game. Several VR games are available via a wide variety of providers, and there is a VR experience at the Baseball Hall of Fame and 360-degree broadcasts of events such as the Home Run Derby in 3D via Virtual Reality.

Not to be left out, Major League Baseball teams are jumping into the fun of Virtual Reality. Try in-stadium VR with the San Francisco Giants or one of the many other teams that are using VR to enthrall their fans even further.

StatCast

One of the biggest advances from MLBAM is StatCast. Before the advent of new tech, baseball was an imprecise game. This is contrary to their image as a game where a fraction of an inch could change everything. For more than 100 years, baseball was called a game of inches when it was actually a game of guessing.

High-tech cameras positioned around the stadium track players throughout the game.

This uncertainty led to years of debates over which players are the best, which players hit the ball harder, and/or what players moved faster in the outfield. They were arguments that were generations old ... until they met StatCast!

All of that information is now readily available due to StatCast.

This revolutionary system has changed baseball forever and allows fans to dig deep into their favorite players' and teams' abilities. This system tracks motion through the high-tech cameras that are strategically placed around the field. It measures nearly every play, error, run, or other event that happens on the field. It then distributes the applicable numbers to fans.

Fantasy baseball would be nowhere without StatCast. In fact, neither would the game of baseball since fans are not the only ones to utilize the information that the StatCast system provides.

Tech for Giving the Players, Trainers, and Statisticians a Better Experience

Players, coaches, trainers, statisticians, managers, owners, and others who shape the game of baseball use wonderful innovative technologies. Every day a new way to measure, view, or upgrade an aspect of the game is dreamt up. Baseball may be America's oldest sport, but it looks brand new.

Smart Tech

Video led the way for the technological explosion in baseball. It not only offers new ways for fans to enjoy the game but is now becoming a player's favorite tool. Beyond what fans have access to, video technology is used to break down and access a player's body mechanics. Players can view footage of their pitching motions, approaches to pitched balls, swings, and more. Players use slow motion or frame-by-frame playback to analyze their performance and learn where they need to improve or adjust their play.

The technology is further enhanced by the use of peripheral add-ons such as sensors. Players can slip a sensor onto their bat to measure multiple aspects of their swing during practice. This tech provides indispensable data that can be combined with video footage to further refine a player's approach.

Pitching mechanics is just one aspect of performance that Smart Tech video technology can help to analyze.

Major League Baseball contracted with the maker of one of these types of sensor—Blast Motion—to offer it to any team that wanted to use it.

New Bat Tech

In recent years, two inventive designs for the bat have been introduced.

The first is the axebat, which is gaining popularity with Major League players. Innovators created the axebat to give the batter a faster swing speed and better control. It is also touted as a way to prevent wrist and hand damage. To achieve these goals, the handle of the axebat is slanted at the end like that of an actual axe.

The second is the Smart Bat. Helpful for improving a batter's technique, the smart bat has a sensor on its base to measure the speed and angle of the swing. Trainers can use the data gathered from the sensor to guide how they train the players.

Virtual Reality

Another tech that is not just for fans is Virtual Reality. The team version is more advanced than that which fans enjoy and can allow players to study their opponent. Furthermore, VR tech allows players to virtually step onto the pitcher's mound, or into the batter's box, or any other

Chicago White Sox pitcher Lucas Giolito watches a training session using virtual reality during spring training.

Demonstration of the new Smart Bat that is sweeping through training camps.

position they want. This gives them the opportunity to view a pitch, hit, catch, foul, or any other part of the game from varied angles and make further assessments about how to approach the situation.

PitchFX and TrackMan

The statistical revolution of baseball demonstrated in the *Moneyball* book and movie led to changes in tech too. Pushing past the traditional methods of evaluating plays by looking at the end result of that play, Major League Baseball now looks to measure what is happening to the ball while it is in play. To reach that end, PitchFX and TrackMan came into Major League Baseball.

In 2006, Major League teams installed sensors in their stadiums. These sensors allow PitchFX to track the physics behind every pitch. This gives teams valuable data that they can use to better utilize the pitcher they have and to find new pitchers who will meet their needs.

The most prominent example of the effect the PitchFX sensors and program has on baseball comes from the Houston Astros. This Major League team employed the tech to take an underappreciated and underutilized pitcher who had already been on two teams and played in fifteen games (Collin McHugh) and make him a more effective player.

The Astros used the PitchFX sensor data to measure data points never before considered. These include:

• How fast a bat strikes a ball

• The spin rate on a batted ball

• The speed with which the ball hits the ground

This close study of McHugh revealed that he had an extreme spin when throwing a curveball. Houston signed him off the Major League Baseball junk pile based on this information. They then fine-tuned his approach using the TrackMan technology while facing down batters to help him become an effective starting pitcher.

TrackMan is available to baseball and softball players at every level. It employs a combination of 3D Doppler radar and innovative video to give instant access to information on important data points similar to the PitchFX system. These systems help to show how to throw a ball without injuring the arm and thus, prolong a pitcher's career.

Houston's Collin McHugh greatly improved his performance following a PitchFX assessment.

Tracking Player Health

Major League Baseball (MLB) teams are deeply invested in the health of their players. Players have their limits. To extend those player limits teams are asking players to wear biomonitors. These unobtrusive devices will assess and document a wide variety of physical data. The wristband monitor tracks an athlete's physical duress and vital signs while resting, sleeping, or doing some activity. Managers and trainers then use the information to adjust sleep cycles, pitching motions, workouts, and running styles.

Teams have experimented with having players wear biomonitors to track vital signs round the clock.

The idea of wearing these trackers during a player's off-hour activities has generated a crucial debate. Issues of privacy and rights enter into the discussion on both sides. Only time will tell how this plays out.

Sleep Rooms

The consideration of a player's health led to teams taking notice of a basic concept that every mother knows … the proper amount of sleep results in better performance. That is why a few teams have outfitted their stadiums with "sleep rooms." These rooms have top of the line mattresses and fresh new bedding and pillows in a relaxing setting to allow players to get the rest they need even at the ball field.

The Future of Baseball Technology

While it may appear that there is no further baseball can evolve, every generation has believed that same thing. The truth is that there is no telling where baseball will go next unless of course, one understands the elements of STEM. That is where the future of humanity lies. Science, technology, engineering, and math are molding a whole new world.

Text-Dependent Questions:

1. How do players use technology to further their skills?

2. How do fans use technology to keep up with their favorite teams?

3. How does Virtual Reality affect the game of baseball?

Research Project:

Think of an advancement for the game of baseball or an area that is lacking and needs improvement or any other place that technology can advance the game of baseball. Research and draft a report detailing why it needs changing, how the new advance can meet that need, and what the projected end result would be. Be creative, inventive, and have some fun.

Acceleration - the rate of change of velocity with respect to time.

Aerodynamics - the branch of mechanics that deals with the motion of air and other gases and the effects of such motion on bodies in the medium.

Algorithm - a set of rules for solving a problem in a finite number of steps.

Amplitude - the absolute value of the maximum displacement from a zero value during one period of an oscillation.

Analytics - the analysis of data, typically large sets of business data, by the use of mathematics, statistics, and computer software.

Biometrics - Methods for differentiating humans based on one or more intrinsic physical or behavioral traits, such as fingerprints or facial geometry.

Center of Gravity - the point at which the entire weight of a body may be considered as concentrated so that if supported at this point the body would remain in equilibrium in any position.

Force - strength or energy exerted or brought to bear.

Geometry - the part of mathematics concerned with the size, shape and relative position of figures, or the study of lines, angles, shapes, and their properties.

Inertia - the property of matter by which it retains its state of rest or its velocity along a straight line so long as it is not acted on by an external force.

Kinetic energy - energy associated with motion.

Mass - the quantity of matter as determined from its weight.

Parabola - a type of conic section curve, any point of which is equally distant from a fixed focus point and a fixed straight line.

Potential energy - the energy of a body or system as a result of its position in an electric, magnetic, or gravitational field.

Velocity - rapidity of motion or operation; swiftness; speed.

FURTHER READING

Adamson, Thomas K. *The Technology of Baseball*. North Mankato, MN: Capstone Publishing, 2017.

Carleton, Russell A. *The Shift: The Next Evolution in Baseball Thinking*. Chicago, IL: Triumph Books LLC, 2018.

Costa, Gabriel B. *Understanding Sabermetrics: An Introduction to the Science of Baseball Statistics*. Jefferson, NC: McFarland & Company, 2008.

Cross, Rod. *The Physics of Baseball and Softball*. Sydney: Springer, 2011.

Fuss, Franz Konstantin. *Routledge Handbook of Sports Technology and Engineering*. New York: Routledge, 2014.

INTERNET RESOURCES

http://www.exploratorium.edu/baseball/index.html
Exploratorium
Exploratorium's Science of Baseball site provides a plethora of tools to explore the insides of the iconic All-American game of baseball. Interactive tools to test reaction time, find a bat's sweet spot, how to throw a slider, why a baseball has stitches, and more.

https://www.mlb.com
Major League Baseball Homepage
Find out all the newest information about the history, players, rules, and other major data about the sport.

https://catcheruniversity.com/
Catcher University
This website, which is dedicated to catchers, states that its mission is to be the comprehensive guidebook to foster excellence in catchers, both off and on the field. It is geared toward players, parents, and coaches alike. The site offers free content through a public electronic library, camps, classes, lessons, and more.

http://thebaseballcatcher.com/
The Baseball Catcher
A thorough source of information geared toward the young catcher. This includes choosing a glove, drills, tips, and more.

INDEX

Aaron, Hank, 51
acceleration, 16, 21, 22
aerodynamics, 8, 9–10, 13
algorithms, 44, 45, 46, 48, 49, 55
aluminum bats, 56, 60, 61–62
angles, 16
    in base running, 39–40, 41
    in catching, 31–32
    in hitting, 17–20, 27
    in throwing, 13
apps for throwing, 15
arcs of balls and runners, 28, 32, 40
Assists (A), 53
automated strike zones, 14
axebat, 71

baseballs
    compression of, 21, 62
    design and standards of, 10, 58–60
    motion of, 10–11, 13, 29–30, 60
Base on Balls (BB), 49, 52
bats, 20–21, 22, 60–62, 71
batters, feedback for, 48–51, 52, 70–71
batting, 17–27
Batting Average (BA), 48–49, 50
batting helmets, 63–64
Beane, Billy, 53
Betts, Mookie, 52
biochemical engineers, 56, 62
biomonitors, 74
Bonds, Barry, 51
breaking pitches, 11, 42
bunting, 26–27

careers, 50, 62
catchers, 29–30, 32–35, 42
catching, 29–35
center of gravity, 36, 39–40
Chapman, Aroldis, 10
Chapman, Ray, 63
cleats, 65
curveball and cutter pitches, 11, 73

diamonds (fields), 40, 58
diving for ball or base, 30, 39

Doak, Bill, 57
drag as force, 8, 9, 10, 12–13

Earned Run Average (ERA), 45, 46–47, 52
equipment, 57–65
Errors (E), 53

fastballs, 10, 11, 17, 60, 62, 64
fastest pitch, 10
fielders, stats for, 53–54
Field-Independent Pitching (FIP), 52
fielding, 12–13, 30–32
Fielding Percentage (FP), 53–54
Finch, Jennie, 47
first base, 39, 42

Giolito, Lucas, 71
gloves, 29–30, 57–58
gravity as force, 9, 10, 12–13
grips on baseball, 11
Guinness Book of World Records, 10

Hamilton, Billy, 38
health of players, tracking of, 74–75
helmets, 63–64
Hit By Pitcher (HBP), 49, 52
hitting, 17–27
home, running for, 40
Houston Astros, 72–73

James, Bill, 53

Keefe, Tim, 46
kinetic energy, 16, 20, 21, 32

left-handedness, 23–25
lift as force, 8, 9, 10, 12
Linear Optical Trajectory (LOT) theory, 30–32
livestreaming of games, 67–68

Maher, Matty, 42
Major League Baseball (MLB), 10, 14, 17, 53, 59–63, 65, 67–68
managers, 53, 54–55
mass, 16, 21

INDEX

math applications, 12, 25, 33–35, 41–43, 45–53
McHugh, Collin, 72–73
MLB Advanced Media (MLBAM), 68–69
MLB.tv, 67
momentum, 16, 20, 23, 32, 39
Moneyball, 50, 53, 72

Nathan, Alan, 39
Newton's First Law, 28, 30

Oakland A's, 50, 53
off-speed pitches, 11, 42–43
On-Base Percentage (OBP), 49, 50, 52
On-Base Plus Slugging (OPS), 50–51
Optical Acceleration Cancellation (OAC) theory, 30–32
outfielders, 12–13, 30–32

Peters, David, 24
physics, 9–10, 12, 20, 29–30, 41
pitch clock, 14
pitchers, feedback for, 14-15, 45–48, 52, 70, 71, 72–73
pitch framing, 33–35
PitchFX, 72–73
pitching, 9–12, 13–15, 17, 24–25, 42–43
Posey, Buster, 32–33
power hitting, 21–22
probabilities, predictions with, 28, 33–35
ProSwing Baseball, 42
Putouts (PO), 53

questions, text-dependent, 15, 27, 35, 43, 55, 65, 75

reaction time, 36, 37–38
research projects, 15, 27, 35, 43, 55, 65, 75
right-handedness, 23–25
running, 37–43
Ruth, Babe, 51

sabermetrics, 44, 51–53
sensors, 70–71, 72–73
shoes and spikes, 64, 65

signal calling, 32, 33–35
situational probabilities, 33
sleep rooms, 74–75
sliding options, 39, 40
Slugging Percentage (SLG), 50
Smart Bat, 71, 72
Smart Tech, 70–71
Society for American Baseball Research (SABR), 51
softball, 17, 40, 62
speed of pitches and hits, 10, 17, 21–22, 73
Statcast, 69
statisticians, 50, 70
statistics, 44, 45–55, 69
stealing bases, 34, 38, 41–43
STEM
        careers in, 50, 62
        scientific concepts of, 7, 9
strike zones, 14
sweet spot of bat, 20–21
swing angle of bat, 17–20

technological innovations, 13–15, 56, 57–65, 66, 67–75
throwing, 9–15
torque in pitches, 8, 11
TrackMan, 72–73
trajectories for catching and running, 28, 30–32, 40
turf, artificial vs. grass, 58

umpires, 14, 34–35

velocity of pitches, 8, 9, 11, 15
videos, 12, 23, 29, 42, 48, 61, 72
Virtual Reality (VR), 66, 68, 71–72

Walks and Hits per Innings Pitched (WHIP), 46, 47
Walsh, Ed, 46
Weighted On-Base Average (wOBA), 52
windup, 9, 10
Wins (W), 47–48
Wins Above Replacement (WAR), 52

Young, Cy, 48

AUTHOR BIOGRAPHY

Aimee Clark is a Freelance Content Writer who has authored several authoritative articles on STEM in education and sports including an extensive manual on extracurricular STEM activities for preteens and teens.

Aimee enjoys learning and sharing what she learns with her readers. She has a Bachelors' Degree in Secondary Education that helps her understand how kids learn. She is also a proud member of the Nonfiction Author's Association (NFAA) and Editorial Freelancer's Association (EFA).

Living in rural Michigan with her husband and four children, the education of children has long been a topic of great personal interest to Aimee, along with helping to further awareness and understanding of our world.

EDUCATIONAL VIDEO LINKS

Pg. 12: http://x-qr.net/1Csv
Pg. 23: http://x-qr.net/1EuR
Pg. 29: http://x-qr.net/1DYP
Pg. 42: http://x-qr.net/1HaH

Pg. 48: http://x-qr.net/1F92
Pg. 61: http://x-qr.net/1Gsz
Pg. 72: http://x-qr.net/1D0B

PICTURE CREDITS